PARKS & MONUMENTS OF THE SOUTHWEST:

New Mexico, Utah, Colorado

Arches National Park BALANCED ROCK

by **Deborahann Smith**

A RENAISSANCE HOUSE PUBLICATION

ISBN: 1-55838-146-5

RENAISSANCE HOUSE
A Division of Jende-Hagan, Inc.
541 Oak Street ~ P.O. Box 177
Frederick, CO 80530

Cover Photo of Fairyland at Bryce Canyon National Park, Utah, courtesy National Park Service.

10 9 8 7 6 5 4 3 2 1

I0809437

WELCOME

Some of the richest land in the United States encompasses the Southwest: mountains, red cliffs, volcanic fields, desert land, unique plant life, intense blue skies, and mighty rivers. Managed by the National Park Service, a diversity of National Parks and Monuments celebrate these areas. They also exist to protect plants and wildlife, to mark historical or geological events, and to preserve ancient cultures. Parks offer great opportunities for us to get in touch with nature and our pasts. But with legitimate concern over the future of the environment, it is important that we practice environmental etiquette during our visits. The rules are simple:

1. *Practice "No trace" ethics.* Remember that everything on an NPS site--even the smallest fossil--is protected by federal law and should be left in place. Pack out trash and use the park's recycling bins when available. Keeping automobile use to a minimum helps the air quality. Use of designated trails prevents erosion. In short, the old adage, *Take nothing but pictures; leave nothing but footprints* is a good rule of thumb.

2. *Watch animals silently, from a distance.* Remember that these areas are their homes. Please don't throw rocks or feed the wildlife. Keep pets leashed, and do not take them into the backcountry.

3. *Respect Indian ruins, and the people who live around them. These* sites not only illustrate cultural history, but are still considered sacred by contemporary Native Americans.

Parks generally charge admission and their hours vary by site and season; it's advisable to call ahead. To learn more about an area prior to visiting, consult these fine guides:

Journey to the High Southwest, Robert L. Casey
Geology of Our Western National Parks & Monuments, Royle C. Rowe

Of related interest in the **Southwest Traveler** series:

The Anasazi
Indian Arts & Crafts
Lost Mines & Buried Treasure

In the **Arizona Traveler** series:

Indians of Arizona
Parks & Monuments of Arizona
Arizona Cactus

CONTENTS

National Park Service ELEPHANT HILL NEEDLES, CANYONLANDS, UT

THE GREAT AMERICAN SOUTHWEST

Have you ever wanted to:
Stand atop a mountain...
Explore deep underground caverns...
Watch dinosaur bones being excavated from a quarry...
Climb to cliff dwellings of prehistoric Indians...
Walk into a volcano...
Hike through a forest of cactus 50 feet tall...
Or walk beneath a 290-foot-high natural stone bridge?

Then you've come to the right place! The American Southwest has all of this to offer and more. Here you can traverse petrified forests and 700-foot-high sand dunes. You can visit a 1500s-style Spanish mission, an 1800s military outpost, and the site of the first Transcontinental Railroad. It is also the only place in the United States where you can put two hands and two feet in four states at once. Four Corners Monument (near the junction of U.S. Highways 191 and 160) marks the alignment of New Mexico, Arizona, Utah and Colorado. Join us on a journey through the southwestern sites that are now commemorated as National Parks, Monuments, Memorials and Historic Sites. We will begin in New Mexico, go north to Utah, and east to Colorado.

National Park Service AERIAL VIEW

Aztec Ruins N.M.

Much as houses are bought and sold today, so were the dwellings at Aztec "recycled." Various Anasazi Indian groups lived here--not Aztecs, as early Anglo settlers who named the site believed. Culturally similar to the Chaco Canyon inhabitants 65 miles south, the first group of Anasazi farmed and hunted along the Animas River. They became skilled at community architecture and masonry work. Their original three-story pueblo, constructed between 1111 and 1115 A.D., was rectangular -- a series of side-by-side inter-connected rooms enclosing a flat, open plaza with a Great Kiva in the center. The pueblo housed 200-300 people in 400-450 rooms. It also contained more than two dozen kivas--ceremonial chambers. By 1200, residents had moved from the area, perhaps because of drought or depletion of natural resources.

About 1225, the dwellings were "remodeled" by another group. Influenced by the Mesa Verde culture of Colorado, these people added rooms and walls, repaired roofs, and introduced variations in kiva styles. They flourished for 50 years, farming and making a distinctive style of pottery as well as textiles. Then they, too, moved, leaving behind a partially burned building.

Aztec, located in northwestern New Mexico, is noted for its numerous ruins within one concentrated area. It has the only reconstructed Great Kiva in the Southwest, accessible from a self-guiding trail. Exhibits of pottery, baskets, and other artifacts of the native people are displayed at the visitor center.

Chris Judson CAVE KIVA

BANDELIER N.M.

Bandelier National Monument is a combination of ancient Pueblo ruins, steep-walled canyons, waterfalls, and undisturbed wilderness. Named for a distinguished Swiss-American scholar who pioneered research here in the late 1800s, it covers nearly 50 square miles. Most of the monument is accessible only on foot. The main stage is the Pajarito (little bird) Plateau, known for its tan cliffs, forested mesas, and deep canyons winding to the Rio Grande. The plateau is comprised mostly of tuff (consolidated volcanic ash) and basaltic lava exploded thousands of years ago by a volcano. The caldera (saucer-shaped impression) created when the volcano collapsed is one of the largest calderas in the world. Its rim forms the Jemez Mountains.

Frijoles (bean) Canyon is accessed by a paved loop trail, and contains 1-1/2-miles of villages carved into cliffs of hardened volcanic ash. Drought forced many southwest Indians to water-dependable areas such as this gorge, cut by a stream that flows high into the mountains. Pueblo farmers, who lived here from 1150 to late 1500 AD, constructed irregularly terraced cliff dwellings, one to three stories high, with many cave rooms carved out of the canyon walls. There people made black-and-white, color, and glazed pottery, and obtained cotton by trade, which they wove into clothing on a loom. Drought, floods, famine, disease, or a

Chris Judson TALUS HOUSE

combination of factors caused them eventually to abandon the area.

Oral traditions link the ancient Pajarito Plateau dwellers with present-day Rio Grande pueblos. Eleven miles north is Tsankawi, a large unexcavated ruin on a high mesa overlooking the Rio Grande valley, Sangre de Cristos, and Jemez Mountains. A 2-mile circle path follows an ancient Indian trail for part of the walk. Many petroglyphs can be seen on the cliffs.

The Bandelier backcountry offers more than 70 trails through rugged and scenic terrain, ranging in duration from 1.5 to 20 miles (45 minutes to 2 days). A popular attraction is the Upper Frijoles Crossing trail to Apache Spring, and Ceremonial Cave, reached by four ladders totaling 140 feet. Other trips include Alamo Canyon, Painted Cave, pueblo ruins of San Miguel and Yapashi, and White Rock Canyon of the Rio Grande, all in a rugged terrain. A map is essential.

Bandelier N.M. is 46 miles northwest of Santa Fe. Camping facilities are available. As budget permits, rangers conduct talks and guided walks to describe the area's archeology, ethnology, and natural history. A side trip takes travelers west to the village of Jemez Springs, site of Indian pueblos, and Jemez State Monument (Franciscan mission ruins, circa 1617). A few miles north is Soda Dam, a 30-foot-high wall built from mineral deposits in the Jemez River. Hot springs bubble out of the river for the next 20 miles, providing a welcome soak for weary travelers.

National Park Service CAPULIN VOLCANO

Capulin Volcano N.M.

Have you ever walked inside a volcano? Capulin *(cah-poo-LEEN)* Volcano is one of the few places where it is possible. Not only does a road spiral to the summit; trails invite you to walk along the rim AND visit the vent at the bottom of the crater! From the rim's highest point, travelers can see Colorado, Oklahoma and Texas.

Capulin is a symmetrical cinder cone that rises 1,000 feet above its base to reach 8,182 feet above sea level. Ten thousand years ago, it played a role in the period of volcanism that had begun two million years before. Volcanic activity is also evidenced in Sierra Grande, 10 miles southeast, and in dozens of surrounding hills and peaks.

Today Capulin is mostly cinders, ash, and rock debris resulting from volcanic eruptions. As forces of nature changed the volcanic matter into soil, its slopes became grassland, evergreen forest, wildflower meadow, and chokecherry-abundant. "Capulin" is Spanish for chokecherry. Porcupines, squirrels, deer, ladybugs, and an occasional golden eagle grace the area.

Capulin is a major landmark of northeastern New Mexico, three miles north of the village of Capulin. Will it erupt again? Only nature knows.

Cavern Supply Co. TEMPLE OF THE SUN

CARLSBAD CAVERNS N.P.

Carlsbad Caverns National Park contains some of the largest series of underground caverns ever discovered. Millions of years ago, more than 300 caves formed in the limestone deposited by an ancient ocean in this area, today called the Guadalupe Mountains. Approximately 80 of these caves have been discovered within park boundaries. Lime-secreting marine organisms created a reef that was buried by many layers of sediment. Carbonic acid-charged rainwater penetrated the rocks, dissolved the limestone, and hollowed out large chambers. Water and minerals entered, drizzling designs on the walls and creating awesome ice formations later named for their shapes and textures: draperies, cave pearls, popcorn, lily pads, soda straws.

Cave tours meander on paved trails through electrically-lit underground chambers. Visitors enter by elevator or through the Natural Entrance, descending to 829 feet below the surface. A major attraction is the cross-shaped Big Room--one of the largest underground chambers in the world. Measuring roughly 1,800 ft. x 1,100 ft. and 255 ft. high, at its highest point, it contains numerous extraordinary formations, including the 62-ft.-high Giant Dome, 42-ft.-high Twin Domes in the Hall of Giants, Mirror Lake, and the Bottomless Pit. Elsewhere in the chamber, other highlights include the Scenic Rooms, which are elaborately decorated with delicate stalactites and marble-like flowstone, and Iceberg Rock, a 200,000-ton boulder that fell from the ceiling thousands of years ago. The Underground

Carlsbad Caverns N.P. THE KLANSMAN

Lunchroom is a place to rest and enjoy a snack. In another cave, a guided lantern tour explores an undeveloped cavern called Slaughter Canyon Cave, featuring the 89-ft.-high Monarch, Christmas Tree column, and the Chinese Wall.

Another popular activity at Carlsbad is bat watching. From early May through October, hundreds of thousands of Mexican free-tail bats burst from the cave entrance at sunset to feed on night-flying insects. The bats winter in Mexico and summer at Carlsbad. Rangers give bat flight talks outside the cavern prior to each evening's flight. For early risers, daily pre-dawn return flights of the bats are equally impressive. Bats make awesome dives from heights of hundreds of feet to re-enter the cave, sometimes at a speed of 25 mph or more. August and September are generally the best bat-viewing months, as baby bats, born in early summer, join the flight. An annual Bat Flight Breakfast is held in August.

Carlsbad Caverns is in SE New Mexico, 20 miles south of the town of Carlsbad. Roadside exhibits and panoramic views are frequent along the 7-mile drive to the visitor center. Day and overnight hikes are offered in the 30,000 acres of sometimes harsh Chihuahuan Desert backcountry wilderness, where summer temperatures can exceed 100°. Ranging in elevation from 3,600 to 6,350 ft., the area is home to a variety of plants, wildlife, and more than 200 species of birds.

National Park Service PUEBLO BONITO

CHACO CULTURE N.H.P.

Chaco Culture is one of the most outstanding archeological areas in the United States. Located in the San Juan Basin, it features 13 major Anasazi ruins in the long, shallow Chaco Canyon, and more than 3,500 archaeological sites within the park's 34,000 acres. For 10,000 years, the Basin has alternately housed Paleo-Indians, Anasazi, Navajos, Spanish-Americans, and Anglos.

Bands of hunters and gatherers first dwelled here. In the 600s, Indian farmers developed irrigation systems, built underground pithouses, and made pottery and intricate basketry. Pueblo culture emerged in the 700s, marked by above-ground dwellings of mud, rock, and poles. Three distinct groups of Anasazi were present in the Southwest at this time: the Mesa Verde in Colorado; the Kayenta in Arizona (now Navajo National Monument); and the Chaco Canyon Anasazi.

Chaco Culture N.H.P. was established to mark the culture of the latter group, which flourished from 900 through 1150. The people of the canyon farmed, made turquoise jewelry, coiled pots, wove sandals, and carved flutes. Their multi-storied structures exhibit finely-detailed masonry. Some dwellings span several acres, containing as many as 800 rooms and circular ceremonial kivas.

The Chaco people may have been connected with the Aztecs of Mexico, at least through trade, since copper bells, feathers of macaws and other parrots, and seashells have been found here. A recent 10-year study

Russ Finley, Chaco Culture N.H.P. ROOMS & KIVA

discovered straight roads going out in all directions from Chaco, indicating that the canyon may have been a hub to major trade routes. The Anasazi abandoned the canyon around A.D. 1200. Navajo Indians reached the area around 1400, but didn't settle Chaco Canyon until the early 1700s. They inhabit much of the surrounding region today.

Chaco Culture N.H.P. is in northwestern New Mexico, accessible by dirt roads off S.H. 57. Sometimes called the "Stonehenge of the West," the ruins are among the largest in the Southwest. Pueblo Bonito, covering three acres, was one of the most substantial structures in the world built before 1887. Five stories high, it contained 800 rooms and 32 ceremonial kivas. The masonry was amazingly precise; the walls resemble tile mosaic. Archeologists are not certain just what function Pueblo Bonito served. It may have been for ceremonial use or for storage, but its primary purpose was not housing.

Chetro Ketl and Pueblo del Arroyo are among other major pueblos at Chaco. Casa Rinconada is an excavated great kiva, one of the most impressive structures in the canyon. All are accessible by one-hour self guiding trails. Museum exhibits and audio programs explaining the history and geology of Chaco Canyon are displayed at the visitor center. Una Vida, a partially excavated ruin, is within a short walking distance. Rangers conduct tours and seasonal evening campfire programs.

National Park Service TRAIL TO INSCRIPTION ROCK

El Morro N.M.

El Morro in western New Mexico, 58 miles southeast of Gallup, preserves more than 700 years of southwestern history, from Anasazi culture through Spanish colonial and American expansion. Situated at a natural water basin near the ancient trail between Zuni and Acoma Indian pueblos, it was a popular campsite for Pueblo Indians, Spanish explorers, Army troopers, and Anglo settlers.

Meaning "The Headland," El Morro was named by Spanish conquistadors during 17-century explorations. The monument's highlight is Inscription Rock, a sandstone monolith on which hundreds of symbols, names, and pictures have been carved by travelers as evidence of their passage. In Zuni, it is "A'ts'ina" - "place of writings on the rock." Follow the 1/2-mile paved Inscription Trail to view an ancient Indian's bighorn sheep depiction, autographs from the 1800s, and several Spanish messages such as "pas* por aqu*" ("passed by here") and Don Juan de Onate's lengthy report of his discovery of the southern seas. Some contemporary visitors can trace their ancestry to names inscribed on the rock.

Mesa Top Trail traverses varied terrain for 2 miles, reaching Anasazi ruins at the top. A museum features exhibits and a video program of the human history of the area. Entrance and camping fees are charged, and trails are restricted to normal hours of operation.

Lydia J. Snell SANDSTONE BLUFF OVERLOOK

El Malpais N.M. & N.C.A.

The national monument named El Malpais *(El Mal-PIE)*, meaning "Badlands," is near Grants, via S.H. 53 or S.H. 117. El Malpais includes a rugged 115,000-acre lava-filled valley with flows from 3,000 to a million years old. Other intriguing features are spatter cones, and a 17-mile lava tube system along C.R. 42.

The area is rich in ancient American Indian history and has a diverse ecosystem. The information center in Grants offers maps to specific areas. Sites along S.H. 117 include Sandstone Bluffs Overlook, with excellent views of the flows, and La Ventana Natural Arch, the largest accessible arch in New Mexico. The Narrows is a corridor created by lava near the base of 500-foot sandstone cliffs. Several unusual lava formations are visible at McCarty's Lava Flow.

Along S.H. 53 is El Calderon, which contains Junction Cave, Twin Craters Lava Flow, El Calderon cinder cone, sandstone formations, and a bat cave. The Zuni-Acoma Trail is an old Pueblo Indian trade route connecting the two pueblos. Once used by Anasazis, this 7-1/2-mile hike crosses four of the five major lava flows. Modern Indians continue their use of the area for cultural and religious purposes. West Malpais Wilderness has a large ponderosa pine parkland surrounded by lava at "Hole in the Wall." Cebolla Wilderness is forested rimrock country.

National Park Service DWELLING ENTRANCE

GILA CLIFF DWELLINGS N.M.

The earliest remains left by the Mogollon (*MUGGY-own*) people along the headwaters of the Gila River are circular pithouses, *ca.* 100-400 A.D. Built in the open, they have underground floors and narrow entrances. The Mogollon architects grew corn, beans, and squash, and also hunted and gathered. Eventually they began constructing masonry villages in open areas along the river near their fields. They became experts at making red-and-brown pottery, using a coiling technique to fashion the native clay.

In the 1270s, a small group of Mogollon began building cliff dwellings into five of Gila's natural caves along the west fork of the Gila River, using masonry and timbers. A total of 40 rooms housed perhaps 10 to 15 families. By the early 1300s they left, perhaps to join other villages north or south. Apaches arrived 100 years later, and Spanish colonists subsequently settled east and south. Their descendants reside here today.

This monument is in southwestern New Mexico, 44 miles north of Silver City. A 1-mile trail loops past the dwellings. The surrounding Gila National Forest and Wilderness boasts two million acres of varied terrain, which incorporates 700 miles of trails, mineral hot springs, a ghost town, and recreation areas.

National Park Service KIVA INTERIOR

Pecos Nat. Hist. Park

Pecos N.H.P. spans 1,000 years of Indian, Spanish, and Anglo culture. Pre-pueblo people first lived here in pithouses around 800 A.D. Pueblo farmers settled in the 100s. Their culture was rich in architecture, crafts, and religion, which emphasized nurturing the spirits of all things--animate and inanimate. By 1450, some 2,000 people inhabited a multi-storied pueblo with more than 20 ceremonial kivas. The exact number of rooms in the pueblo is not known, but 660 have been excavated. Because of its location, guarding a large mountain pass, Pecos became a major trade center.

Coronado's gold-seekers reached Pecos in 1541, followed by Spanish explorers. A Franciscan mission was founded by 1598. Pueblos and Spaniards lived fairly peacefully until 1680 when the Indians rebelled against Catholic conversion by destroying the mission; but the Franciscans returned 12 years later. In 1838, 17 remaining Pecos people emigrated to Jemez Pueblo where their descendants live today. Archeologist A.V. Kidder began excavations in the area in 1915.

Pecos is in north-central New Mexico, 25 miles SE of Santa Fe. A 1-1/4-mile scenic trail leads through mission and pueblo ruins and two kiva interiors. On summer weekends, native Americans and Hispanics demonstrate traditional crafts.

Fort Union N.M.

NICK EGGENHOFER PAINTING: "Wagon Train at Wagon Mound"

Fort Union Nat. Mon.

Fort Union preserves the ruins of an important Santa Fe Trail fort, considered one of the largest military posts in the west. Established in 1851 when the U.S. Army relocated its headquarters out of Santa Fe, it was a principal quartermaster depot that served as a station for military activities, including defense from Indian tribes. Fort Union also had its own arsenal and supplied other regional forts.

The Civil War in 1861 sparked fear of a Confederate invasion of New Mexico, prompting the construction of a new earthwork fort. Fort Union avoided direct attack, but its soldiers were involved in battles that helped secure New Mexico's place in the Union. The fort was again rebuilt in 1863 but abandoned in 1891 after the completion of the Santa Fe Railroad.

Fort Union is in NE New Mexico, 28 miles NE of Las Vegas. Exhibits illustrate its colorful history; foot trails are equipped with audio messages. The fort is part of the National Historic Santa Fe Trail, which covers 900 miles of present-day Missouri, Kansas, Colorado, Oklahoma, and New Mexico. The trail played an important role in the western expansion of the U.S. and was a major route for commerce before the railroads. Along the trail are buildings, historic markers, and the intriguing remains of wagon wheel ruts worn into the earth by the pioneers.

National Park Service QUARAI RUINS

Salinas Pueblo Missions N.M.

Salinas Pueblo Missions consists of three large Pueblo Indian villages and four Franciscan stone churches. As at Pecos, Indians settled the Salinas Valley centuries before the Spaniards arrived, inhabiting first pithouses, then apartment-like buildings. Both Anasazi and Mogollon had roots here as far back as 7,000 years ago, preceded by more ancient nomadic tribes approximately 13,000 years earlier. The Mogollon were well-established by the 10th century. Anasazi came in the late 1100s, and emerged as the dominant culture by 1300.

Although these people weren't as sophisticated as Pueblos to the north, this became one of the most populated parts of the Pueblo world. Located between major trade routes, the salt-rich Salinas Valley itself evolved as an important trade center. Villagers traded maize, pinyon nuts, beans, squash, salt, and cotton goods for dried buffalo meat, hides, flints, and shells.

Spanish explorers appeared in the 1500s, bringing wheat, fruit trees, cattle, goats, and metalwork, all welcomed by the Indians. When Franciscan missions introduced Christianity, however, the natives were skeptical. Pueblo religion relied on many spirits and gods to bring rain, seed fertility, and dependable harvests. Could the white man's god do all of this single-handedly? In the end, this cultural difference, plus natural disasters, diseases, and Apache raids, weakened the Salinas pueblos. Both pueblos and missions were abandoned during the 1670s.

This national monument is located in central New Mexico, in three separate sections near Mountainair.

National Park Service GYPSUM DUNE

White Sands N.M.

White Sands is just that--glistening dunes of white sand up to 60 feet high--the world's largest gypsum dune field. It lies in the Tularosa basin, surrounded by the San Andres Mountains to the west and the Sacramento Mountains to the east. These "striped" mountains are layers of dark shale and light limestone containing gypsum, which most people know as "plaster of Paris." Gypsum differs from other sand because it is water-soluble, like sugar or salt. When rain falls on the mountains, some of the gypsum dissolves and is carried into the basin. Because there is no river to wash it away, the gypsum remains in puddles where it falls. As the puddles evaporate and gypsum dries, it forms fragile crystals called selenite. Battered by wind and rain, the selenite breaks into minute grains of sand.

Wind must move at least 15 mph to pick up sand. The winds here normally blow from the southwest, moving the dune field slowly to the northeast. Only the most well-adapted life forms can survive in such a harsh environment. Some of White Sands' numerous small creatures have evolved sand-coloration as protection from predators.

White Sands is in south-central New Mexico, 52 miles east of Las Cruces. There is an eight-mile scenic drive into the dunes. Big Dune Trail is a one-mile self-guided trail.

National Park Service DELICATE ARCH

Arches National Park

Driving the 21 miles of paved roads that wind through Arches National Park, travelers can get the unmistakable feeling of being in a bizarre movie. Everywhere you look are enormous red stone arches and contorted monoliths, with names like Dark Angel, Three Gossips, Sheep Rock, and Parade of Elephants. Here is the country's largest group of natural stone arches, spires, windows, and pinnacles, some of them hugging the roadside.

About 150 million years ago, these formations were actually sand. The sand formed into cemented layers of rock that were lifted and cracked; erosion converted the masses into their present sandstone shapes. Their red coloration indicates the presence of iron oxide, which is responsible for most of the red rocks in Utah's "canyon country."

A 21-mile paved road is a popular way to tour the park; there are several viewpoints, parking areas, and short trails along the way. Beginning at the visitor center, the road passes the Courthouse Towers, Petrified Dunes, and the Great Wall enroute to other park sections. Trails provide access to the formations. Nestled among cliffs and slickrock domes, the famous Delicate Arch is reached via a 1.5-mile walk. Within view are the canyon walls of the Colorado River and the peaks of the La Sal Mountains. The arch can also

National Park Service LANDSCAPE ARCH

be viewed from a distance at the Delicate Arch Viewpoint, located across the canyon. The Windows section is a great place for casual walks. Scenic Park Avenue is an easy 1-mile walk (one way) through a deep-walled corridor. Landscape Arch, one of the longest natural arches in the world, can be viewed on the Devils Garden Trail. This trail features eight large arches and other formations.

Each day in season, naturalists guide visitors through a maze of redrock fins to the Fiery Furnace area. The half-day hike to Klondike Bluffs, a remote area of the park, is a hit with backcountry adventurers, for here is the site of the enormous Tower Arch and the Marching Men formations. Four-wheel-drive or mountain bike roads throughout the park provide access to beautiful desert and wilderness areas.

Arches is set on 73,000 acres in southeast Utah, 5 miles north of Moab on U.S. 191. Elevations range from 4,085 to 5,653 feet in this sparse pinyon-juniper community, typical of the Great Basin desert.

Museum exhibits, films, talks, literature, and maps are available at the visitor center, and guided walks are given seasonally. Both the park and outlying areas offer camping and picnic facilities.

Located on the Colorado River, Moab is the jumping-off point for a variety of side trips into other areas of canyon country via horse, boat, jeep, mountain bike, and foot. Be sure to investigate Dead Horse Point State Park, 30 miles away, for panoramas reminiscent of the Grand Canyon.

National Park Service FAIRYLAND

BRYCE CANYON N.P.

Bryce Canyon National Park hosts 1.5 million annual visitors from all over the world. One section of the park is known as Fairyland, for its red, pink, orange and brown limestone pinnacles called "hoodoos." The hoodoos are also found in other areas of the park. Air quality here is excellent, with more than 100 miles of visibility and a wealth of starry nights. The park has an air quality monitoring program and photographic monitoring station for visibility.

Located on a high section of the Colorado Plateau, Bryce's elevation ranges from 6,600 to 9,100 feet. The formations were created by an accumulation of sand, silt, and lime that washed into inland lakes and compacted into layers of rock. The land was later uplifted to mountain-sized heights, and erosion shaped it into the present-day rock patterns.

An 18-mile main road and four major spur roads lead to the park's 13 overlooks, of which Fairyland, Sunrise, Sunset, Inspiration, and Bryce points are the most popular. Surrounding forests, meadows and breaks provide habitat for a variety of plants and animals. Hiking trails vary from the relatively short 1-mile Bristlecone Loop to the strenuous 8-mile Fairyland Loop. A backcountry trail extends 22 miles under the rim. Bryce is in southwestern Utah, near U.S. 89.

National Park Service CONFLUENCE

CANYONLANDS NATIONAL PARK

The Colorado and Green Rivers divide Canyonlands's 527-sq.mi. into four distinct districts of innumerable canyons, spires, mesas, buttes, and arches on the Colorado Plateau. These geologic formations are the result of a large area of continental crust's being subjected to rock building and erosion over millions of years. An interesting feature here is a black, knobby substance called cryptobiotic soil. Comprised of a combination of organisms, it holds moisture, prevents erosion, and adds nitrogen and carbon to the shallow soil. The thin crust is very fragile and shouldn't be walked on. Humans have inhabited this harsh area intermittently for 10,000 years, living beneath cliff overhangs, crafting spearheads, and leaving ghost-like drawings on the walls. They have come and gone as the desert climate and natural resources deemed the region survivable.

"Island in the Sky" district, 6,000 ft. above sea level, is a high, level mesa--the place to go if you have limited time. Several overlooks offer breathtaking views of the White Rim, Needles, and Maze districts, as well as of distant mountain ranges. Visitors can drive one or all of the paved roads, and choose from short hiking trails to Upheaval Dome, Crater View, Mesa Arch, or Grand View. For those with more time and endurance, White Rim Road is a 102-mile 4WD loop around Island in the Sky. Trips usually take two to three days by 4WD or three to four days by mountain bike.

(Continued on pg. 26)

NEW MEXICO

UTAH

COLORADO

Please refer to *Parks & Monuments of Arizona* in the **Arizona Renaissance Travelers Series** for information about the parks and monuments of that state

0 20 40 60 80 100

0 50 100 150 Ki

NATIONAL
PARKS AND MONUMENTS
of
NEW MEXICO,
UTAH and COLORADO
WYOMING
COLORADO
UNION PACIFIC
CONTINENTAL
DIVIDE
Routt National Forest
Roosevelt National Forest
Estes Park
Rocky Mountain National Park
Craig
Greeley
Brush
Loveland
Boulder
Denver
White River National Forest
White River National Forest
Pike National Forest
Limon
Kit Carson
Grand Mesa National Forest
Gunnison National Forest
Black Canyon of the Gunnison National Monument
Gunnison
San Isabel National Forest
Florissant Fossil Beds National Monument
Colorado Springs
Bent's Old Fort National Historic Site
Pueblo
Montrose
Curecanti National Recreation Area
Rio Grande National Forest
San Isabel National Forest
DENVER & RIO GRANDE
Arkansas
SANTA FE
La Junta
Great Sand Dunes National Monument
Rio Grande National Forest
Walsenburg
Alamosa
Trinidad
Durango
COLORADO
NEW MEXICO
Raton
Capulin Volcano National Monument
Aztec Ruins National Monument
Carson National Forest
Taos
Santa Fe National Forest
Bandelier National Monument
Santa Fe National Forest
Fort Union National Historic Site
Pecos National Historic Park
Chaco Culture National Historic Park
Santa Fe
Conchas Lake
Canadian
National Forest
Albuquerque
Santa Rosa
SOUTHERN PACIFIC
El Malpais National Monument
Salinas Pueblo Missions National Monument
Rio Grande
Cibola National Forest
Socorro
Pecos
Lincoln National Forest
Alamogordo
Gila Cliff Dwellings National Monument
White Sands National Monument
Lincoln National Forest
Las Cruces
Carlsbad
Carlsbad Caverns National Monument
NEW MEXICO
N

Canyonlands N.P. MONUMENT BASIN, ISLAND IN THE SKY

"The Needles" is an apt description of this district of colorful rock spires. Popular for day hikes and backpacking, trails range from easy 30-minute walks to such places as Roadside Ruin, Pothole Point, and Cave Spring, to strenuous overnight hikes like Lower Red Lake and Upper Salt Creek. Other trails access the Confluence Overlook, Elephant Hill, Druid Arch, and backcountry trips to Angel Arch and Devil's Kitchen Loop. The Salt Creek Archaeological District offers Indian ruins and rock art.

The region known as "The Rivers" refers to the Colorado and Green, which wind through steep-walled canyons and meet near the center of the park. Cataract Canyon, a 14-mile stretch of treacherous whitewater, is popular with seasoned boaters.

Look for solitude, silence, and challenge in the Maze, the most remote Canyonlands district. Trails and four-wheel-drive roads lead to Land of Standing Rocks, the Doll's House and Ernies Country. The Maze itself is a labyrinth of canyons that can be reached only on foot. Horseshoe Canyon is a detached area of the park that boasts some of the best prehistoric rock art in the country.

Canyonlands N.P. is in southeastern Utah near Moab. Detailed information and maps are available through the Island, Maze, and Needles Districts. The park has several campgrounds, picnic areas, and dirt roads for mountain biking. Spring through fall, rangers offer campfire talks and guided walks.

National Park Service CAPITOL REEF

Capitol Reef National Park

"Land of the Sleeping Rainbow," the Navajo name for Capitol Reef, is a national park where all colors of the rainbow can be seen in the rocks. Millions of years ago, this area was covered by a shallow sea that receded, deposited varicolored sediments and minerals, and hardened into rock layers. Powerful forces collapsed and slanted the rocks to create the "Waterpocket Fold," the geologic structure that characterizes Capitol Reef. Hiking is a major activity here and there is a walk for everyone, ranging from the easy 1-mile Capitol Gorge trail to the strenuous 4-1/2-mile Navajo Knobs. Other trails offer rim-walks, natural bridges, and panoramic views.

The 378-square mile park is located in south-central Utah, "the heart of Canyon Country," on S.H. 24, halfway between Canyonlands and Bryce Canyon. From May to September, free guided walks and evening programs in the outdoor amphitheater are offered. Nearby historic Fruita features a restored schoolhouse and implement shed, remnants of the Mormon pioneer community that settled here in 1880. Tape-recorded messages describe life in an early Mormon community and teaching in a one-room schoolhouse. When in season, visitors may pick fruit at the apple, cherry, pear, peach, and apricot orchards, illustrating how the area got its name.

Zion Natural History CEDAR BREAKS

Cedar Breaks N.M.

Cedar Breaks National Monument preserves a natural rock amphitheater more than 2,000 feet deep and 3 miles in diameter, on the edge of the 10,000-foot Markagunt Plateau. Within the amphitheater are brilliant red, yellow and purple stone spires, columns, arches and canyons, posed like statues in a multitude of shapes. The result of the same forces that formed the Grand Canyon, Zion and Bryce Canyon, Cedar Breaks was created by millions of years of uplift and erosion. Its colors are from the iron and manganese deposits.

Called "Circle of the Painted Cliffs" by early Indians, later Utah pioneers dubbed it Cedar Breaks--"cedar" for the cedar trees, and "breaks," a synonym for badlands. Above the amphitheater is the high country, a land of spruce-fir forests, subalpine wildflower meadows, and an abundance of birds and wildlife.

Cedar Breaks is in southwestern Utah, via S.H. 143. It features a 5-mile scenic drive with four overlooks, and three highcountry trails. The Alpine Pond Trail loops to a forest glade and spring-fed pool. The Ramparts Trail traverses the plateau rim, passing ancient bristlecone pines at Spectra Point (one specimen is over 1600 years old), and ends with a view of the amphitheater. The Rattlesnake Creek Trail, north of the park, is for more seasoned hikers.

National Park Service "JUPITER" and "119"

GOLDEN SPIKE NATIONAL N.H.S.

Golden Spike National Historic Site commemorates the building of the nation's first Transcontinental Railroad. On May 10, 1869, the Union Pacific and Central Pacific joined here as two locomotives pulled up to a one-rail gap in the track. The Golden Spike Ceremony symbolized its completion with the driving of the Golden Spike, which was dropped into a pre-drilled hole and tapped ceremoniously with a silver plated maul. The last spike was actually of the standard iron variety, driven with a regular maul. After this important binding of East and West, the two steam engines, "Jupiter" and "119," began their return journeys.

This project was constructed by approximately 20,000 workers, mostly Chinese from the west as well as Civil War veterans and European immigrants from the east. Mormon settlers did the grading for both railroads in Utah. The teams laid 2 to 5 miles of track a day, Central Pacific beginning in January 1863 and Union Pacific in the fall of 1865. The railroad drastically changed the country. A wagon journey of 6 months was now accomplished in a few days by train. Actual time from Omaha to Sacramento was 4 days, 7 hours. Settlements grew around the railroad stations. Trade via rail transformed the economy, as east and west took advantage of each other's resources.

Golden Spike is 32 miles west of Brigham City, Utah. Along the original roadbed, 1.6 miles of track have been relaid and exact replicas of the "Jupiter" and "119" operate during the summer.

National Park Service SIPAPU, NATURAL BRIDGES

Natural Bridges N.M.

Natural bridges were created millenia ago when the land across which streams meandered suddenly rose, causing the water to cut deep channels in the sandstone. As the streams bent back upon themselves, they undercut the canyon walls until only a thin fin of stone separated them. Flash floods pounded against the weak spots formed by soft layers in the sandstone, and eventually the water cut through the narrow neck of the meander, forming a natural bridge.

The monument preserves three bridges, each from a different geologic phase. The stream that formed the oldest, Owachomo, has abandoned its original course, leaving the bridge at the mercy of gravity. Sipapu, in the mature stage of its development, has widened beyond the water that flows beneath it. Periodic flash floods still attack the abutments of Kachina, the youngest.

The bridges originally were named Edwin, Augusta, and Caroline, for early explorers. But in 1908, after the land was made a national monument, Indian names were adopted. "Owachomo" refers to the "rock mound" above the eastern abutment of the bridge. Augusta was renamed "Sipapu", the gateway through which Hopi spirits enter or leave the world. Caroline bridge became "Kachina" for petroglyphs found both beneath the bridge and on kachina dancers' costumes.

Natural Bridges is 40 miles west of Blanding, along S.H. 95. The 9-mile Bridge View Drive accesses overlooks and trailheads to the bridges. Additional canyon trails lead to archeological sites representing a blend of Mesa Verde and Kayenta Anasazi culture.

Glen Canyon N.R.A. RAINBOW BRIDGE N.M.

RAINBOW BRIDGE N.M.

Rainbow Bridge, the largest natural bridge in the world, spans 275 feet, and arches to a height of 290 feet. The top is 42 feet thick and 33 feet wide. Its salmon color has dark iron oxide or hematite stains called "desert varnish" which sparkle in the afternoon sun. The upper part of the bridge is composed of easily eroded Navajo sandstone. The base is Kayenta sandstone--consolidations of reddish-brown or purple layers of sands and muds laid down hundreds of millions of years ago. This is a harder rock, not so easily cut by running water. Both formations were buried more than 5,000 feet deep by strata over the next 100 million years, then hardened by pressure and heat. Rainbow Bridge is sacred to many native Americans.

Rainbow Bridge is located amid a network of canyons between Navajo Mountain and the Colorado River. Before the impoundment of Glen Canyon and the creation of Lake Powell, it was in one of the most inaccessible areas in the United States. Today most visitors access Rainbow Bridge by water. It's 50 miles from Wahweap, Bullfrog, or Halls Crossing to Bridge Canyon, then a 1/4- to 3/4-mile walk to the monument. There are also trails from the abandoned Rainbow Lodge or from Navajo Mountain Trading Post (13 and 14 miles respectively). Since this is Navajoland, hiking permits are required from the Navajo Nation.

National Park Service ARAGONITE CRYSTAL

Timpanogos Cave N.M.

High on the rocky slopes of American Fork Canyon sits Timpanogos Cave National Monument, containing three underground limestone caverns. Formed nearly 4 million years ago, they weren't discovered until 1887-1921. What makes these caves special is the numerous exotic formations called "helictites," uncommon in other caves. Less than 1/4-inch in diameter, helictites are fragile as hand-blown glass. Unlike stalactites, which hang like icicles, and stalagmites that grow up from the floor, helictites twist in many directions, defying gravity. These and other crystals seem to light up the cave's interior, reflecting in underground pools. "Flowstone," "draperies," and "cave popcorn" make up the Cascade of Energy, Chocolate Fountain, Frozen Sunbeam, and other crystal formations. Rarely a cave cricket, bat, or other creature of the dark may appear.

Timpanogos is southeast of Salt Lake City, off I-15. Couch potatoes, beware! The cave entrance is via a 1.5-mile trail that zigzags 1,065 feet up the steep wall of American Fork Canyon. Benches are provided along the way for breath-catching and breathtaking views of the canyon, Wasatch Range, and Utah Valley. The caves are connected by man-made tunnels; tours are ranger-guided.

Bob Clemenz THE WATCHMAN

Zion National Park

Centuries of rain, wind, freezing, and the Virgin River's driving force have eroded Zion into wonderful rock patterns, deep canyons, and spectacular 2,000-3,000-foot cliffs. Because Zion has more than 5,000 feet of elevation change, visitors are also treated to the richest diversity of plants found in Utah--more than 800 species--brightly contrasted against the orange-red cliffs. Colorful names hint at what travelers see.

Highlighted is the Zion Canyon Scenic Drive (13 miles round trip), which winds through this southwestern Utah canyon past Mountain of the Sun, the Great White Throne, and Angels Landing. From the central section of the park, forested Lava Point offers a view of Kolob Terrace highlands. The Zion-Mt. Carmel Highway connects lower Zion Canyon with the high eastern plateaus via two narrow tunnels. On one side is the Great Arch of Zion, carved high into a cliff wall; on the other side is Checkerboard Mesa, mountain that has cracked and eroded into hundreds of fantastic shapes.

Hiking trails at Zion range from easy to strenuous. The Gateway to the Narrows Trail is so popular that more than 700,000 people walk it annually. This easy 2-mile hike along the river features trailside exhibits and hanging gardens of wildflowers in spring and summer.

Victor Jackson — ANGELS LANDING

Another easy trail (1/2-mile) leads to more hanging wildflower gardens and to Weeping Rock, a rock alcove with dripping springs. Lower Emerald Pool is an easy to moderate 1.2-miles to a pool and waterfalls during the spring. Travelers with more time can hike in the river to Orderville Canyon. A strenuous 14-mile hike through orange-red Kolob Canyons ends at Kolob Arch, one of the world's largest-known free standing arches. Other trails surprise hikers with spectacular views of Zion Canyon, a desert swamp, Anasazi ruins, ancient rock art, and cabin sites from the 1880s.

Situated on nearly 230 sq. mi., Zion N.P. is located in south-central Utah. The Zion Canyon Visitor Center, 1/2-mile from the south entrance near Springdale, Utah offers a museum, introductory slide show, books, maps, permits for backcountry hiking, and a nearby nature center. A few miles north is Zion Lodge which provides lodging, a restaurant, guided tram tours, and a hiker shuttle service. Information is also available at the Kolob Canyons Visitor Center in the northwest corner of the park. Park rangers offer an abundance of free activities such as guided walks, interpretive talks, and evening programs at the campground amphitheaters. Topics include geology, plants, animals, history, archeology, and Zion's night sky.

National Park Service CANNON & BELFRY

BENT'S OLD FORT N.H.S.

Bent's Old Fort was a powerful frontier hub during the early 1800s. It was built by two brothers, Charles and William Bent, and Ceran St. Vrain, who quickly befriended several Indian tribes and Mexican traders. To strengthen ties with the Indians, William Bent married Owl Woman, daughter of a powerful Cheyenne priest. He also encouraged rival tribes to tolerate one another, and so the fort operated in an atmosphere of peace. By trading manufactured goods for pelts and furs, Bent, St. Vrain and Company soon made this fort the most important port of call between Independence, Missouri and Santa Fe, New Mexico. From here, American trade and influence made its way south to Mexico, west to the Great Basin, and north into Wyoming.

In 1846, the annexation of Texas brought U.S. troops to the fort as a jump-off point for invasion into New Mexico. Trade came to a halt as soldiers entered into conflict with the Indians. The added misfortune of a cholera epidemic among the Indians caused William Bent to abandon the fort. He later built a new trading post--Bent's New Fort--38 miles down the Arkansas River.

Bent's Old Fort eventually was reconstructed so travelers could experience its historical flavor. It is located in southeastern Colorado, 8 miles east of La Junta, and 15 miles west of Las Animas on S.H. 194.

National Park Service RIM VIEW

Black Canyon Of The Gunnison & Curecanti

Black Canyon is the 53-mile-long work of a powerful sculptor, the Gunnison River, 12 miles of which comprise Black Canyon of the Gunnison N.M. Named for its walls of dark rock, it ranges in depth from 1,700 to 2,700 feet, with 1,150-ft.-wide Narrows. It took 2 million years to form the present canyon; many rocks here are 1.7 billion years old, some of the oldest exposed rocks on earth. The most spectacular views are along the gravel North Rim Drive, east of Crawford, where the canyon walls are almost vertical. The 7-mile South Rim Drive features 12 overlooks, and several foot trails, varying from an easy few hundred feet to 2 miles. One trail ends with a view of the famous Painted Wall, the tallest cliff in Colorado.

This is a nesting area for the peregrine falcon, one of the last shelters in Colorado for this endangered species. Mule deer, yellow-bellied marmot, infrequent bighorn sheep, and a variety of other wildlife can also be seen. Seasoned hikers can try the strenuous Inner-Canyon trip, which requires a permit.

Black Canyon of the Gunnison is in west-central Colorado, 15 miles east of Montrose, via U.S. 50 and S.H. 347. The North Rim closed in the winter; South Rim roads are plowed to Gunnison Point. Nearby Curecanti National Recreation Area is a trio of reservoirs upstream on the Gunnison River. Set against a landscape that exploded out of volcanic activity 30 million years ago, it offers trails and water sports galore.

Rick Nolan KISSING COUPLE

COLORADO N.M.

Colorado National Monument is a 32-sq. mi. treasury of deep canyons, awesome rock sculptures, pinyon woodlands and a limited number of desert springs. Rising more than 2,000 feet above the Colorado River's Grand Valley, the monument is part of the Colorado Plateau, which also embraces the geologic wonders of the Grand Canyon, Bryce Canyon, and Arches. Working here over millions of years, nature's artists sculpted and painted such monoliths as Pipe Organ, the Kissing Couple, Sentinel Spire, and the Praying Hands. The area's establishment as a monument was largely the effort of one man, John Otto, who lived alone in canyon country during the early 1900s, and built many of the trails. Wrote Otto, "I came here last year and found these canyons, and they felt like the heart of the world to me."

Rim Rock Drive winds 23 miles, from Grand Valley to the park's high country. It skirts the plateau's rim, serving up panoramas of rock sculptures, distant valleys and mountains. Several short self-guiding trails cut through the canyons and woodlands. The longer Serpents Trail is more strenuous. Nicknamed "the Crookedest Road in the World," it has 50 switchbacks. Colorado National Monument is west of Grand Junction, via I-70.

National Park Service CAST SKELETON OF ALLOSAURUS

Dinosaur National Monument

One hundred fifty million years ago, this land was alive with vegetarian dinosaurs--Brontosaurus, Diplodocus, Stegosaurus, and their carnivorous predator, Allosaurus. After they died, floodwaters washed some of the carcasses into a sandbar. As more sediment covered the sandbar, their bones were preserved in the sand, along with the remains of turtles, crocodiles, and clams.

For millions of years this area was like an underground museum, filled with bone deposits as they mineralized. When the Rocky Mountains were formed to the east, the area rode along with them, being squeezed up from the sides to create today's Dinosaur Quarry--the place in the park to view dinosaur bones. One wall of the quarry is enclosed so that travelers may view 1,600 fossil dinosaur bones.

Dinosaur National Monument is not only about dinosaurs. It is also embraced by wilderness and canyons cut by the Green and Yampa rivers. The Harpers Corner Scenic Drive travels into the heart of canyon land. A 1-mile trail at the end of the road overlooks numerous canyons.

Backcountry travelers will want to drive the 13-mile Echo Park Road. Since this is river country, rafting is one of the best ways to view the area. The monument borders northwest Colorado and northeast Utah at U.S. 40, and S.H. 149 at Jensen.

Walt Saenger HORNET HYMENOPTERA

FLORISSANT FOSSIL BEDS N.M.

Florissant Fossil Beds harbors the fossilized impressions of dragonflies, beetles, spiders, butterflies, fish, mammals, and birds. Among them are 1,100 insect species, 140 plant species, and most of the fossilized butterflies in the New World. There are also petrified tree stumps. Where did all these specimens come from?

This impressive collection was preserved in sedimentary rock at the bottom of a 30-million year old lake. Lake Florissant was formed when lava from the nearby Thirtynine Mile volcanic field dammed streams that flowed through the valley. Volcanic eruptions over another 500,000 years subsequently sprayed millions of tons of ash, dust, and pumice into the air. Much of this wind-carried material settled over and around Lake Florissant, trapping a variety of plants and animals. Some were carried to the lake bottom, buried in fine ash that turned to shale, then fossilized. Trees caught in volcanic mudflow also were petrified. Over millions of years, these items were gradually exposed through erosion.

Florissant ("flowering" in French) was probably named for its magnificent wildflower meadows, by an early settler who established a Ute Indian trading post here after the Civil War. The monument includes a museum, nature and hiking trails, picnic areas, and an historic 1870s homestead. It is located in central Colorado, about 35 miles west of Colorado Springs on U.S. 24.

National Park Service DUNES

GREAT SAND DUNES N.M.

The traveler's first impression is a tawny sea of sand, but actually these are North America's tallest sand dunes. Rising up 700 feet from the desert floor of the San Luis Valley, they make a dramatic contrast to the deep blue sky, surrounding golden desert and forestland, and the blue-blacks of towering mountain ranges. The dunes are bordered on three sides by the Sangre de Cristo Mountains, San Juans, and San Luis Hills. Formation began when the Rio Grande deposited sediment as it flowed through the San Luis Valley 2 million years ago; it continues today. Fine grains were picked up by southwest winds and dropped at the foot of the Sangre de Cristo Range. Dunes formed when pebbles and gravel trapped the wind-blown sand, piling it into small mounds.

Humans are known to have lived in the area since 15,000 B.C. Spearheads and bone findings prove that a tribe of hunters camped just west of the dunes 10,000 years ago, and had a campfire supper of bison. Several Indian groups, explorers, and settlers followed.

Great Sand Dunes National Monument is located in south-central Colorado, 34 miles from Alamosa. it is great fun to hike or slide on the dunes. Travelers may also walk or 4WD along Medano Creek which borders the dunes on the east. The 1/2-mile Montville Nature Trail is north of the visitor center.

Art Hutchinson CLIFF PALACE

Mesa Verde N.P.

The most renowned cliff dwellings in the U.S. are at Mesa Verde, Colorado. Dating from the late 1100s, these elaborate stone cities were built by a group of pre-Columbian native Americans now called the Anasazi. Fashioned from breadloaf-sized sandstone rocks, cemented together with mud and water, they range from one-room houses to the famous 217-room Cliff Palace. Archeologists believe that many of the walls were once plastered and painted with designs.

As a culture, the Anasazi went through distinct life-style changes. The first, called the Basketmakers after their basketry skills, settled Mesa Verde (Spanish for "green table") in pithouses about A.D. 550. Their baskets were finely and tightly woven. Waterproofed with pitch, they were used for carrying water, storing grain, and even cooking.

Basketry declined with the advent of pottery, which was probably crafted by the community's women. Black-on-white vessels of all kinds were used for ceremonial and everyday use; personal designs were handed down from mother to daughter. Archeologists are still looking at reasons why the Anasazi began living above ground in the mid-700s, and became known as Pueblos, Spanish for "village dwellers". More sophisticated masonry evolved around 1000 A.D. Later, during the 1200s, advanced construction techniques resulted in the spectacular cliff houses at Mesa Verde National Park.

The Anasazi hunted, gathered, and farmed. Their

Mesa Verde N.P. COURTYARD, SPRUCE TREE HOUSE

tools were skillfully shaped from stone, bone, and wood. An important part of their economy was the domestic turkey, which provided food, feathers for weaving, and bones for tools. Mesa Verde's population may have reached several thousand between 1100 and 1300. In the late 1200s they began moving south, perhaps driven by drought into present-day New Mexico and Arizona. Some of today's Pueblo Indians are their descendants.

Anasazi architectural development is apparent along Ruins Road on Chapin Mesa, including Spruce Tree House, Cliff Palace--the largest cliff dwelling in the park--and the tallest and most photogenic ruin, Square Tower House. Summer visitors can hike the 2.8-mile Petroglyph Point Trail and the 2.1- mile Spruce Canyon Trail. More remote Wetherill Mesa has summer access via a 12-mile mountain road. It features the mesa-top Badger House Community and Long House, a long plaza used for dances and village ceremonials. Step House ruins have both subterranean houses of the Modified Basketmakers (*ca* 600) and pueblos from the Classic Pueblo period (*ca* 1200).

Mesa Verde's entrance is 10 miles east of Cortez and 36 miles west of Durango. An archeological museum on Chapin Mesa has artifacts and exhibits. Far View Visitor Center displays contemporary Indian arts and crafts. Cliff dwellings and other remains are explained at wayside exhibits throughout the park. Park Service employees also provide a variety of interpretive programs, tours, and seasonal campfire talks.

Dale Coker MOONRISE OVER THE CASTLE

HOVENWEEP N.M.

Hovenweep National Monument preserves six groups of Pueblo Indian ruins, culturally similar to the Mesa Verde inhabitants. The Anasazi lived in the Four Corners area until almost A.D. 1300. For centuries these people occupied small, scattered villages in open valleys and mesa tops.

Around 1200 they moved to the Hovenweep canyons which contained permanent springs. Here they hunted, gathered, and grew crops, including corn, beans and squash. Known as talented artisans and craftsmen, they constructed pueblos and towers, notable for their square, oval, circular, and "D" shapes. Some were built on boulders or rim edges. A long drought forced the Hovenweep dwellers to desert the area by the late 1200s.

Hovenweep (Ute for "deserted valley") borders southern Utah and Colorado, 45 miles from Cortez. The Square Tower Group in Utah--best preserved and most impressive--is accessible via a self-guided trail. Cajon Ruin (Utah) and the Holly, Hackberry, Horsehoe, Cutthroat Castle, and Goodman Point Ruins (Colorado) are more isolated.

Jerry Cleveland ROCKY MOUNTAIN NATIONAL PARK

Rocky Mountain N.P.

Believe it or not, this scenic high-mountain park was once a vast ocean. When the ocean receded more than 100 million years ago, mountains rose gradually out of the original sea bed. Erosion by wind and water over several million years produced the Rocky Mountains. Ice created enormous glaciers that formed lakes, moraines, and U-shaped valleys. Five glaciers can be seen in the park today.

More than 100 miles of paved roads and 355 miles of trails wind through the 415-sq.mi. Rocky Mountain N.P. There are 114 named peaks above 10,000 ft. and 91 peaks top 11,000, including the famous 14,255-foot Longs Peak. The park also contains 147 lakes. Trail Ridge Road, the highest continuously paved road in the U.S., is a spectacular drive that crosses the Continental Divide. Trail Ridge climbs to more than 12,000 feet and stays above tree line for 11 of its 50 miles. It is open from late May through mid-October, depending on weather.

Hiking is a major activity in areas with names like Chasm Lake, Chaos Canyon, and the Never Summer Range. Bear Lake is the jump-off point for a number of trails ranging from easy nature paths to more strenuous highcountry hikes. The Emerald Lake Trail to Nymph, Dream and Emerald Lakes is popular. Trails also lead

Stanley Zamonski ALBERTA FALLS

to Flattop Mountain, Longs Peak, Lake Helene, and Tyndall and Andrews glaciers. People often ski and sled on this eternal icebowl in July and August. Chasm Falls, the Convict Cabins (historical ruins), and Willow Park (a wildflower/wildlife meadow) are other attractions here. Wildlife includes bighorn sheep, mule deer, wapiti (American elk), and 260 species of birds, among them the endangered bald eagle. Coyotes, black bears, mountain lions, and bobcats are also native to the park. Moose are frequently seen in the Kawuneeche Valley.

Rocky Mountain N.P. is in north-central Colorado, 65 miles northwest of Denver via US 34 or 36. Entrances are at Grand Lake and Estes Park. There are a number of picnic areas, and both front country and backcountry campgrounds. Grand Lake, the largest glacial lake in the state, is the site of regattas, and boasts "The World's Highest Yacht Club." Check the visitor centers at Estes Park and Grand Lake, and at Fall River Pass for exhibits, detailed information about the park, and ranger-guided programs. If your visit is in the summer, expect a bit of company. It is common to have as many as 3,500 visitors and employees within this popular area on a single summer night!

National Park Service SALINAS PUEBLO MISSIONS N.M.

NAMES & NUMBERS

Arches N.P.
PO Box 907
Moab, UT 84532
801-259-8161

Aztec Ruins N.M.
P.O. Box 640
Aztec, NM 87410
505-334-6174

Bandelier N.M.
Los Alamos, NM 87544
505-672-3861

Bent's Old Fort N.H.S.
35110 Highway 194 East
La Junta, CO 81050
719-384-2596

Black Canyon of the Gunnison Natl. Mon.
2233 E Main - Suite A
Montrose, CO 81401
303-249-7036

Bryce Canyon N.P.
Bryce Canyon, UT 84717
801-834-5322

Canyonlands N.P.
125 W 200 South
Moab, UT 84532
801-259-7164

Capitol Reef N.P.
HC 70; Box 15
Torrey, UT 84775
801-425-3791

Capulin Volcano N.M.
Capulin, NM 88414
505-278-2201

Carlsbad Caverns N.P.
3225 Natl. Pks. Hwy.
Carlsbad, NM 88220
505-785-2232

Cedar Breaks N.M.
P.O. Box 749
Cedar City, UT 84720
801-586-9451

Chaco Culture N.H.P.
Star Route 4, Box 6500
Bloomfield, NM 87413
505-786-7014

Colorado N.M.
Fruita, CO 81521
303-858-3617

Curecanti N.R.A.
102 Elk Creek
Gunnison, CO 81230
303-641-2337

Dinosaur N.M.
Box 210
Dinosaur, CO 81610
303-374-2216

El Malpais N.M.
201 E. Roosevelt
Grants, NM 87020
505-285-4641

Rick Nolan COLORADO NATIONAL MONUMENT

NAMES & NUMBERS

El Morro N.M.
Route 2, Box 43
Ramah, NM 87321
505 783-4226

Florissant Fossil Beds N.M.
P.O. Box 185
Florissant, CO 80816
719 748-3253

Fort Union N.M.
Watrous, NM 87753
505 425-8025

Gila Cliff Dwellings N.M.
Route 11, Box 100
Silver City, NM 88061
505-536-9461

Golden Spike N.H.S.
P.O. Box 897
Brigham City, UT 84302
801-471-2209

Great Sand Dunes N.M.
Mosca, CO 81146
719-378-2312

Hovenweep N.M.
McElmo Route
Cortez, CO 81321
303-529-4465

Lake Mead N.R.A.
601 Nevada Hwy.
Boulder City, NV 89005
702-293-8906

Mesa Verde N.P.
Mesa Verde N.P., CO 81330
303-529-4465

Natural Bridges N.M.
Box 1
Lake Powell, UT 84533
801-259-5174

Pecos N.H.P.
P.O. Drawer 418
Pecos, NM 87552
505-757-6032

Rainbow Bridge N.M.
c/o Glen Canyon N.R.A.
Box 1507
Page, AZ 86040
602-645-2511

Rocky Mountain N.P.
Estes Park, CO 80517
303-586-2371

Salinas Pueblo Missions N.M.
Box 496
Mountainair, NM 87036
505-847-2585

Timpanogos Cave N.M.
RR #3, Box 200
American Fork, UT 84003
801 756-5238

White Sands N.M.
P.O. Box 1086
Holloman AFB, NM 88330
505-479-6124

Zion N.P.
Springdale, UT 84767
801-772-3256

Arizona's National Parks & Monuments

Canyon de Chelly N.M.
P.O. Box 588
Chinle, AZ 86503
602-674-5436

Casa Grande Ruins N.M.
1100 Ruins Drive
Coolidge, AZ 85228
602-723-3172

Chiricahua N.M.
Dos Cabezas Route, Box 6500
Willcox, AZ 85634
602-824-3560

Coronado Natl. Memorial
4101 E Montezuma Cyn. Rd.
Hereford, AZ 85615
602-366-5515

Fort Bowie N.H.S.
P.O. Box 158
Bowie, AZ 85605
602 847-2500

Glen Canyon N.R.A.
P.O. Box 1507
Page, AZ 86040
602-645-2471

Grand Canyon N.P.
P.O. Box 129
Grand Canyon, AZ 86023
602-638-7888

Hubbell Trading Post N.H.S.
P.O. Box 150
Ganado, AZ 86505
602-755-3475

Montezuma Castle N.M.
P.O. Box 219
Camp Verde, AZ 86322
602-567-3322

Navajo N.M.
HC71, Box 3
Tonelea, AZ 86044
602-672-2366

Organ Pipe Cactus N.M.
Route 1, Box 100
Ajo, AZ 85321
602-387-6849

Petrified Forest N.P.
Petrified Forest N.P., AZ 86028
602-524-6228

Pipe Spring N.M.
Moccasin, AZ 86022
602-643-7105

Saguaro N.N.
3693 S Old Spanish Trail
Tucson, AZ 85730
602-883-6366

Sunset Crater N.M.
2717 N. Steves Blvd.
Flagstaff, AZ 86004
602-527-7042

Tonto Natl. Mon.
HC02, Box 4602
Roosevelt, AZ 85545
602-467-2241

Tumacacori N.M.
Box 67
Tumacacori, AZ 85640
602-398-2341

Tuzigoot N.M.
P.O. Box 219
Camp Verde, AZ 86322
602-634-5564

Walnut Canyon N.M.
Walnut Canyon Rd.
Flagstaff, AZ 86004
602-526-3367

Wupatki N.M.
2717 N Steves Blvd.-#3
Flagstaff, AZ 86004
602-527-7040

For a complete description of these sites, refer to
THE RENAISSANCE TRAVELER:
Parks & Monuments of Arizona,
also by Deborahann Smith and published by
Renaissance House Publishers.